The Power of Social Media:

A Comprehensive Guide to Gaining Followers and Unlocking Benefits

Kay Julius

DEDICATION

I dedicate this to all everyone working effectively to give voice to the voiceless across the globe.

TABLE OF CONTENTS

ACKNOWLEDGMENT

I extend my appreciation to my clients, followers and fans who have helped to sharpen my knowledge and expansive experience in this field, and to all those who made this publication possible.

PREFACE

Welcome to the world of social media, where connections are forged, communities are built, and influence knows no bounds. In this digital era, social media has emerged as a powerful tool that can propel individuals and businesses to new heights of success. At the heart of this phenomenon lies a fundamental element: followers.

This book is a comprehensive guide that delves into the strategies, insights, and secrets behind acquiring a large and engaged following on social media platforms. Whether you're an aspiring influencer, a business owner seeking to expand your reach, or simply someone who wants to harness the power of social media, this book is your roadmap to success.

In the following chapters, we will explore a wide array of strategies and techniques that have proven effective in cultivating a thriving social media following. From understanding the nuances of different platforms to crafting compelling content, from leveraging the influence of others to nurturing genuine engagement, we will provide you with the tools and knowledge to navigate the dynamic landscape of social media.

But this book is more than just a collection of tactics. It is a call to action—a call to embrace the transformative potential of social media and to unlock the possibilities that lie within. In these pages, you will find inspiration from real-life success stories of individuals and businesses that have harnessed the power of social media followers to achieve remarkable results.

However, it is important to note that building a substantial following requires time, effort, and patience. There are no overnight miracles or shortcuts to success. Instead, we will guide you through a step-by-step process that emphasizes authenticity, consistency, and meaningful connections. We will equip you with the knowledge and strategies needed to build a loyal following that not only amplifies your voice but also supports your endeavors.

It is our hope that this book will empower you to embrace social media as a platform for self-expression, creativity, and influence. We invite you to embark on this journey with an open mind and a willingness to learn. Whether you are a novice or an experienced social media user, there is always room for growth and improvement.

As you immerse yourself in the chapters that follow, remember that building a strong social media following is not just about the numbers—it is about forging genuine connections, providing value to your audience, and inspiring others through your unique perspective. It is about leveraging the power of social media to make a positive impact in the lives of others and to fulfill your own aspirations.

So, let us embark on this exciting adventure together. Get ready to unleash the power of social media followers and discover the limitless possibilities that await you. Your journey starts now.

Kay Julius (2023)

Chapter One

Social Media: The Digital Revolution

Social media platforms have revolutionized the way people connect, share information, and engage with each other. Over the past two decades, these platforms have undergone substantial changes, shaping different facets of our personal lives, business strategies, and even political landscapes. In this comprehensive article, we will delve into the transformation and impact of social media platforms, exploring their emergence, key milestones, and their influence on society.

Birth of Social Media Platforms

The origins of social media can be traced back to the early days of the internet. Platforms such as Six Degrees, which debuted in 1997, enabled users to create profiles and connect with others. However, it wasn't until the early 2000s that social media platforms gained significant traction. Friendster (2002) and MySpace (2003) introduced features like friend connections and customizable profiles, attracting millions of users and laying the foundation for future platforms.

The Ascent of Major Social Media Platforms

The mid-2000s saw the rise of several influential social media platforms. Facebook, launched in 2004, swiftly gained popularity among college students and eventually expanded worldwide. Twitter, founded in 2006, introduced microblogging and real-time updates, while YouTube (2005) transformed video sharing. Additionally, platforms like LinkedIn (2003) catered to professional networking, serving the business community.

The Mobile Revolution and Social Media

The advent of smartphones and mobile internet access played a pivotal role in social media's evolution. Platforms like Facebook, Twitter, and Instagram (2010) developed dedicated mobile apps, enabling users to connect and share content on the go. Mobile-centric features like location-based services and multimedia capabilities enriched the user experience, leading to widespread adoption.

Expansion of the Social Media Landscape

Social media expanded beyond its early pioneers. Snapchat (2011) introduced ephemeral messaging, while platforms like Pinterest (2010) and Tumblr (2007) focused on visual content sharing. WhatsApp (2009) and WeChat (2011) revolutionized instant messaging, and TikTok (2016) popularized short-form video content. These platforms catered to specific niches, diversifying online engagement.

Impact on Communication and Relationships

Social media platforms have redefined how people communicate and maintain relationships. They offer instant, real-time communication, breaking down geographical barriers. Individuals can connect with friends, family, and colleagues, fostering a sense of community. However, concerns have arisen about social media's impact on mental health, privacy, and interpersonal relationships' quality.

Influence on Information Sharing and News Consumption

Social media platforms have become significant sources of news and information. They enable rapid content sharing, democratizing information dissemination. Nevertheless, this has also led to challenges like misinformation spread, filter bubbles, and echo chambers. The role of social media in shaping public opinion and influencing political discourse has become a subject of intense debate.

Impact on Business and Marketing

Social media platforms have transformed business practices and marketing strategies. They provide businesses with potent tools to engage with customers, build brand awareness, and drive sales. Influencer marketing has gained prominence, utilizing social media personalities for product and service promotion. Moreover, platforms like LinkedIn have become indispensable for professional networking and recruitment.

Social Activism and Political Movements

Social media has played a pivotal role in facilitating social activism and political movements. Platforms like Twitter have been instrumental in organizing protests, raising awareness, and mobilizing communities. Movements like the Arab Spring, Black Lives Matter, and #MeToo have gained momentum through social media, underscoring its potential for societal change.

Privacy and Ethical Concerns

The evolution of social media has raised significant privacy and ethical concerns. Issues such as data privacy, security breaches, and the exploitation of user information by third parties have become pressing. Social media platforms have faced scrutiny over their handling of user data and their algorithms' potential for manipulation and polarization.

Future Trends and Challenges

The future of social media platforms holds both opportunities and challenges. The integration of emerging technologies like virtual reality, augmented reality, and artificial intelligence may reshape how we interact and engage on these platforms. Addressing concerns related to privacy, misinformation, and online harassment will be vital to ensure a positive and inclusive social media environment.

Conclusion

Social media platforms have undergone profound evolution since their inception, leaving a lasting impact on various aspects of society. They have revolutionized communication, information sharing, business strategies, and activism. While these platforms have brought numerous benefits, they also present challenges related to privacy, mental health, and misinformation. As we move forward, navigating these challenges and shaping social media platforms to promote meaningful connections, inclusivity, and responsible use is essential.

The Importance of Social Media for Individuals and Businesses

Social media has ingrained itself into our daily routines, reshaping the way people and businesses communicate, connect, and engage with the world. This article will delve into the significance of social media platforms for both individuals and businesses, emphasizing the advantages and possibilities they present.

Significance for Individuals

a. Communication and Connectivity

Social media platforms offer swift and convenient communication, enabling people to connect with friends, family, and acquaintances across geographical borders. Through messaging, comments, and content sharing, individuals can uphold relationships, exchange experiences, and stay updated on each other's lives.

b. Information and Knowledge Sharing

Social media serves as a vast repository of information and expertise. Individuals can access news, articles, tutorials, and educational content shared by others. Platforms like Facebook, Twitter, and LinkedIn also facilitate the exchange of ideas and knowledge, enabling individuals to learn from experts and engage in meaningful discussions.

c. Personal Branding and Networking

Social media platforms provide opportunities for personal branding and self-expression. Individuals can exhibit their talents, skills, and achievements through profiles, portfolios, and content sharing. Platforms like LinkedIn offer a space for professional networking, connecting individuals with peers, mentors, and potential employers, enhancing career prospects and opening doors to new opportunities.

d. Social Causes and Activism

Social media has emerged as a potent tool for raising awareness, rallying support, and advocating for social causes. Platforms like Twitter and Instagram empower individuals to amplify their voices, share narratives, and engage in dialogues that drive positive change. Social media serves as a platform for activism, enabling individuals to endorse and partake in movements and campaigns addressing diverse social issues.

Significance for Businesses

a. Brand Awareness and Exposure

Social media platforms have become indispensable for businesses in establishing brand recognition and exposure. By crafting engaging content and leveraging features such as posts, stories, and videos, businesses can reach a broader audience and enhance their visibility. Social media allows businesses to showcase their products, services, and values, forging a robust brand identity and attracting potential customers.

b. Customer Engagement and Relationship Building

Social media empowers businesses to interact directly with their customers, nurturing meaningful relationships. Platforms like Facebook, Twitter, and Instagram offer features like comments, likes, and direct messages that facilitate two-way communication. By addressing customer queries, feedback, and concerns, businesses can cultivate trust, loyalty, and customer contentment.

c. Targeted Marketing and Advertising

Social media platforms equip businesses with potent tools for precise marketing and advertising. With comprehensive user data and analytics, businesses can pinpoint their target audience and develop personalized campaigns. Features like ad targeting, retargeting, and lookalike audiences enable businesses to reach the right audience with relevant content, optimizing the efficacy of their marketing endeavors.

d. Market Research and Insights

Social media platforms deliver valuable insights into consumer behavior, preferences, and trends. Through social listening and analytics, businesses can gather real-time feedback, monitor industry discussions, and detect emerging market trends. This data can inform business strategies, product development, and customer-centric decision-making.

e. Competitive Advantage and Collaboration

Social media furnishes businesses with a competitive edge by facilitating the monitoring and learning from competitors. Businesses can scrutinize competitor profiles, campaigns, and customer interactions to gain insights and adjust their own strategies accordingly. Social media also fosters collaboration and partnerships, enabling businesses to connect with influencers, industry experts, and complementary brands for mutual growth.

Conclusion

Social media platforms have become indispensable for both individuals and businesses. For individuals, social media offers avenues for communication, knowledge sharing, personal branding, and opportunities for social activism. For businesses, social media provides channels for brand awareness, customer engagement, targeted marketing, market research, and collaboration. Grasping and harnessing the potential of social media can yield numerous benefits and opportunities in our interconnected world.

Overview of Prominent Social Media Platforms and their Distinctive Characteristics

Social media platforms have transformed the way we connect, share information, and engage with others in the online realm. Each platform presents a unique array of features and functionalities, catering to diverse user preferences and requirements. This article will provide an overview of some well-known social media platforms and emphasize their distinctive attributes.

Facebook

Facebook stands as the largest social media platform globally, with billions of active users. It primarily focuses on connecting individuals and facilitating social interactions. Key elements of Facebook include:

Profiles and News Feed: Users create personal profiles featuring photos, posts, and personal details. The News Feed displays updates from friends, pages, and groups.

Friends and Groups: Users can establish connections with friends, participate in or create groups based on shared interests, and share content within these networks.

Pages: Businesses, public figures, and organizations can create pages to interact with their audience through posts, videos, events, and customer reviews.

Instagram

Instagram centers on visual content, particularly photos and videos, and has garnered significant popularity, especially among younger demographics. Key features of Instagram encompass:

Feed and Stories: Users share photos and videos in their feed, viewable by their followers. Instagram Stories, ephemeral content lasting 24 hours, offer a more informal and real-time sharing experience.

Filters and Editing Tools: Instagram offers a wide array of filters and editing tools to enhance the visual appeal of photos and videos.

Explore Page: The Explore page suggests content based on user preferences, enabling users to discover new accounts, trends, and popular posts.

IGTV and Reels: IGTV facilitates longer-form video content, while Reels allows users to craft short, entertaining videos with special effects and music.

Twitter

Twitter, renowned for its real-time updates and concise format, serves as a microblogging platform, emphasizing swift information sharing, conversations, and trending topics. Key features of Twitter encompass:

Tweets and Retweets: Users can share brief messages, known as tweets, with their followers. Retweeting permits users to disseminate others' tweets to their own followers.

Hashtags: Hashtags assist in categorizing and discovering tweets related to specific topics or events. Users can follow hashtags to **stay updated on discussions.**

Mentions and Replies: Users can mention other users in their tweets using the "@" symbol to engage in conversations and direct communication.

Trends: Twitter showcases trending topics, spotlighting the most popular discussions and hashtags at any given time.

LinkedIn

LinkedIn is a professional networking platform tailored for career advancement, business connections, and industry-related discourse. Key features of LinkedIn comprise:

Professional Profiles: Users craft professional profiles spotlighting their work history, skills, and education. LinkedIn serves as an online resume and networking tool.

Connections and Recommendations: Users can connect with colleagues, mentors, and industry professionals. They can also provide and receive recommendations to showcase their **expertise and credibility.**

Job Listings: LinkedIn offers a robust job portal where users can search for job opportunities, apply directly, and connect with recruiters.

Groups and Content Sharing: LinkedIn groups offer spaces for professionals to engage in industry-specific conversations, share insights, and build connections.

YouTube

YouTube reigns as the world's premier video-sharing platform, offering a vast repository of user-generated and professional content. Key features of YouTube comprise:

Video Uploads: Users can upload and share their videos, establishing their channels to cultivate an audience and monetize their content.

Subscriptions and Recommendations: Users can subscribe to channels and receive updates on new video uploads. YouTube suggests videos based on users' viewing history and preferences.

Comments and Engagement: Users can comment on videos, partake in discussions, and interact with content creators and fellow viewers.

Live Streaming: YouTube provides live streaming capabilities, permitting users to broadcast real-time content and engage with their audience via chat.

These are merely a few examples of prominent social media platforms and their distinctive attributes. Each platform offers a unique experience, catering to varied user interests, demographics, and objectives. Understanding these platforms and their features can empower individuals and businesses to effectively leverage social media for communication, networking, marketing, and content dissemination

11

Chapter Two

Crafting an Effective Social Media Strategy

Before immersing yourself in the realm of social media and embarking on your quest to gain followers and reap its rewards, it's paramount to establish your goals and objectives. Clearly defining your goals provides you with direction, focus, and a roadmap for your social media strategy. In this chapter, we will delve into the significance of setting your goals and objectives and offer practical guidance on how to do so effectively.

The Importance of Goal Setting

a. Strategic Clarity

Defining your goals helps you align your social media initiatives with your overarching business or personal objectives. It ensures that your social media actions contribute to the broader mission and vision you have established for yourself or your organization. By maintaining a clear focus, you can make informed decisions, allocate resources efficiently, and gauge progress accurately.

b. Measurement and Assessment

Establishing specific goals enables you to measure and evaluate the success of your social media endeavors. Without well-defined objectives, it becomes challenging to ascertain whether your efforts are yielding the desired results. Clear goals empower you to track key performance indicators (KPIs), gauge the efficacy of your strategies, and make data-driven adjustments for optimizing outcomes.

c. Motivation and Accountability

Setting goals provides motivation and a sense of purpose. When you possess a lucid vision of what you aim to accomplish through social media, it becomes simpler to remain committed and driven. Furthermore, sharing your goals with others, whether it's a team or your social media followers, fosters a sense of accountability and motivates you to stay on course.

Steps to Establishing your Goals and Objectives

a. Identify Your Purpose

Commence by comprehending why you wish to harness the potential of social media. Is it to promote your business, raise awareness about a cause, establish yourself as an industry authority, or connect with a specific audience? Clarifying your purpose will guide you in establishing pertinent and meaningful goals.

b. Specify Your Goals

Vague goals are challenging to measure and achieve. Strive for precision by delineating precisely what you intend to accomplish. Instead of expressing a general desire like, "I want to gain more followers," stipulate a specific target number, such as "I aim to increase my follower count by 20% within six months."

c. Ensure Measurability

Measurable goals allow you to monitor progress and assess success. Define metrics that align with your objectives, such as follower counts, engagement rates, website traffic referrals, lead generation, or conversion rates. These quantifiable metrics offer tangible indicators of your social media performance.

d. Set Realistic and Achievable Goals

While aspiring for grand achievements is essential, it's equally important to establish goals that are realistic and attainable. Consider your available resources, time constraints, and the current state of your social media presence. Establishing unattainable goals may lead to frustration and a decline in motivation, so strike a balance between ambition and feasibility.

e. Establish a Timeline

Attach a timeframe to each goal to introduce a sense of urgency and structure. Whether it's short-term objectives (monthly or quarterly) or long-term goals (annual or multi-year), having a timeline will help you maintain focus and accountability. Break larger goals into smaller milestones to facilitate more effective progress tracking.

f. Align Goals with Your Target Audience

Factor in the needs and preferences of your target audience when formulating your goals. Ensure that your objectives align with what your audience finds valuable and engaging. By comprehending their desires and motivations, you can tailor your content and strategies to attract and retain their attention.

g. Periodically Review and Adjust Goals

Social media is a constantly evolving landscape, necessitating regular review and adjustment of your goals. Analyze your progress, evaluate the effectiveness of your strategies, and adapt to evolving trends, shifts in audience behavior, and alterations in industry dynamics. Flexibility and adaptability will be instrumental in staying relevant and maximizing your social media impact.

Conclusion

Defining your goals and objectives stands as a pivotal step in unlocking the potential of social media. It furnishes strategic clarity, facilitates measurement and evaluation, and keeps you motivated and accountable. By adhering to the steps outlined in this chapter, you can establish clear and actionable goals that will guide your social media endeavors and enable you to attain your desired outcomes. Remember to periodically review and revise your goals as you progress on your social media journey.

Discovering your Target Audience

One of the foundational pillars of a successful social media strategy is the ability to comprehend and effectively pinpoint your audience. Identifying your target audience empowers you to customize your content, messaging, and engagement tactics to resonate with the appropriate individuals. In this chapter, we will delve into the significance of identifying your target audience and provide practical guidance on how to do so adeptly.

The Importance of Identifying Your Target Audience

a.   Relevant and Compelling Content

Understanding your target audience equips you to craft content that is pertinent, valuable, and captivating to them. By grasping their demographics, interests, preferences, and pain points, you can create content that directly addresses their needs and aspirations. This amplifies the chances of grabbing their attention, cultivating a devoted following, and fostering meaningful engagement.

b. Efficient Resource Allocation

Identifying your target audience assists in the efficient allocation of your resources. By concentrating your efforts on the right audience segments, you can optimize your time, budget, and energy. Instead of dispersing your efforts indiscriminately, you can focus on platforms, channels, and strategies aligned with your audience's inclinations and behaviors.

c. Enhanced Conversion Rates

When you comprehend your target audience, you can tailor your messaging and calls-to-action to resonate with them. This elevates the likelihood of transforming your social media followers into customers, subscribers, or advocates. By delivering targeted content and offers, you can nurture trust, credibility, and a sense of connection that propels conversions and augments your bottom line.

Steps to Identifying Your Target Audience

1. Define Your Product or Service

Initiate the process by defining what you offer and the issue it resolves. Grasp the fundamental features, benefits, and unique selling points of your product or service. This clarity will guide you in identifying the audience that can derive the greatest benefit from what you have to offer.

2. Conduct Market Research

Meticulous market research is indispensable for the identification and comprehension of your target audience. Employ a blend of primary and secondary research techniques to accumulate insights. Primary research may encompass surveys, interviews, or focus groups with existing customers or potential target audience members. Secondary research entails the examination of industry reports, competitor analyses, and social media listening tools to attain a comprehensive understanding of your market.

3. Create Buyer Personas

Buyer personas are fictitious representations of your ideal customers. Based on your research, identify shared characteristics, demographics, behaviors, and motivations within your target audience segments. Assign each persona a name, age, job title, and personal background to humanize them. This exercise deepens your insight into your audience and directs your content creation and engagement strategies.

4. Analyze Your Existing Audience

If you already maintain a social media presence, scrutinize your current audience to glean insights. Leverage analytics tools provided by social media platforms to comprehend the demographics, interests, and engagement patterns of your present followers. This data can corroborate or fine-tune your buyer personas and steer your content strategy moving forward.

5. Harness the Power of Social Listening

Social listening entails the monitoring and analysis of online conversations and dialogues associated with your industry, niche, or brand. Employ social listening tools to identify trends, sentiments, and topics that resonate with your target audience. This information can guide your content creation, engagement tactics, and even product development.

6. Solicit Audience Surveys and Feedback

Engage directly with your audience via surveys, polls, or feedback forms to amass valuable insights. Pose questions regarding their preferences, challenges, and expectations. This firsthand information can assist you in refining your target audience profiles and aligning your strategies accordingly.

7. Refine and Iterate

Identifying your target audience is an ongoing endeavor. As your business evolves and market dynamics shift, revisit your buyer personas and audience profiles at regular intervals. Remain abreast of industry trends, consumer behaviors, and social media platform advancements. Continually refine and iterate your strategies to ensure they stay attuned to your target audience's evolving requirements and inclinations.

Conclusion

Identifying your target audience constitutes a pivotal stride in harnessing the potential of social media. It empowers you to produce pertinent content, optimize resource allocation, and enhance conversion rates. By adhering to the steps delineated in this chapter, you can attain an in-depth comprehension of your target audience's demographics, interests, and motivations. This knowledge will steer your content creation, engagement strategies, and overarching social media approach, allowing you to connect with the right audience and unlock the benefits of social media for your business or personal brand

Choosing the Appropriate Social Media Platforms for your Goals

In the expansive realm of social media platforms, it's imperative to pick the ones that align with your objectives and the audience you wish to target. Each platform possesses distinct features, user demographics, and engagement styles, underscoring the importance of selecting those best suited to your goals. In this chapter, we will delve into the process of choosing the right social media platforms and use examples to illustrate their suitability for specific objectives.

Understanding Platform Characteristics

1. Facebook

Facebook, the largest social media platform, boasts a diverse user base spanning various age groups and demographics. It's well-suited for businesses and individuals aiming to establish a broad online presence, engage with a wide audience, and share diverse content formats such as text, images, videos, and links. Robust advertising options on Facebook make it ideal for brands seeking to reach a vast audience and drive conversions.

Example: A clothing brand targeting diverse age groups, aiming to raise brand awareness and boost sales, can benefit from a presence on Facebook. They can showcase their products through visually appealing images and videos, interact with their audience through comments and shares, and utilize Facebook ads for precisely targeted promotions.

2. Instagram

Instagram, a visually oriented platform centered on photo and video sharing, predominantly attracts a younger audience, making it suitable for businesses and individuals targeting millennial and Gen Z. Instagram shines when it comes to displaying products, lifestyle content, and visual storytelling. Features like Instagram Stories and IGTV enhance the interactive content experience.

Example: An interior design influencer can harness Instagram to share captivating photos of exquisitely designed spaces, offer tips and inspiration, and engage with their audience through comments and direct messages. They can collaborate with brands through sponsored posts, showcasing products that align with their aesthetic and style.

3. Twitter

Twitter, a microblogging platform renowned for real-time updates and concise messaging, appeals to journalists, thought leaders, and individuals eager to engage in public discourse. Twitter excels in delivering timely news updates, fostering industry discussions, and serving as a platform for thought leadership content. Its use of hashtags and retweets enables content to reach a broader audience.

Example: A tech expert or consultant can employ Twitter to share industry news, insights, and engage in conversations with thought leaders and professionals. They can participate in relevant hashtag discussions, provide quick tips and recommendations, and establish themselves as a trusted source for industry-related information.

4. LinkedIn

LinkedIn, a professional networking platform focused on business and career-related content, caters to professionals, B2B companies, and job seekers. LinkedIn offers avenues for thought leadership, industry networking, and the dissemination of educational content. It excels at building professional relationships, showcasing expertise, and generating leads.

Example: A business consultant aiming to establish thought leadership in their field can leverage LinkedIn to share insightful articles, dispense practical advice, and engage with professionals through comments and messages. Joining relevant LinkedIn groups and participating in discussions can expand their network and attract potential clients.

5. YouTube

YouTube, a video-sharing platform boasting a vast and diverse user base, accommodates various content genres. It suits content creators, educators, and businesses that can harness video content to engage their audience. YouTube's monetization options through ads and sponsorships make it appealing to individuals and brands eager to generate income from their content.

Example: A fitness trainer can create a YouTube channel to share workout routines, nutritional guidance, and motivational content. They can provide comprehensive video demonstrations, engage with their audience through comments and live chats during workouts, and monetize their channel through brand collaborations and advertisements.

As we have explained in the previous notes, in selecting the Right Platform for Your Objectives, you must:

Define Your Goals

Initiate the process by clearly articulating your social media objectives. Are you aiming to boost brand recognition, generate leads, drive sales, establish thought leadership, or connect with a specific audience? Each goal may necessitate a different platform or a combination thereof.

Comprehend Your Target Audience

Delve into the demographics, interests, and behaviors of your target audience. Research their most active platforms and align your choices with their preferences. This approach will streamline your options, enabling you to focus on platforms where you can effectively reach and engage your audience.

Evaluate Platform Features

Scrutinize the distinctive features, formats, and capabilities of each platform. Consider whether the platform's content format (e.g., images, videos, text) aligns with your content strategy and objectives. Assess the available advertising options, analytics tools, and engagement features to pinpoint platforms that best support your goals.

Factor in Resource Allocation

Assess the resources at your disposal, including time, budget, and content creation capabilities. Some platforms demand more time and effort for content creation and maintenance. Evaluate your capacity to consistently produce and engage on a specific platform before committing to it.

Conclusion

Selecting the appropriate social media platforms plays a pivotal role in effectively reaching and engaging your target audience. By comprehending the unique characteristics and suitability of various platforms, defining your objectives, and considering your audience's preferences, you can make informed decisions regarding platform prioritization. Remember to periodically reassess and adapt your platform choices as your goals and audience evolve. Leveraging each platform's strengths empowers you to harness the potential of social media to achieve your objectives and reap its benefits.

Creating an Effective Content Strategy for Connecting with your Audience

Crafting captivating content plays a pivotal role in leveraging the potential of social media. Nevertheless, not all content is equal, and it's imperative to devise a content strategy that strikes a chord with your audience. In this chapter, we will delve into the process of creating a content strategy that effectively captivates your intended audience and yields meaningful outcomes. Throughout this chapter, we will employ examples to elucidate crucial concepts.

Understanding Your Audience

- **Audience Research**

Initiate by conducting comprehensive audience research to gain insights into their demographics, interests, preferences, and pain points. Employ social media analytics, surveys, and customer feedback to comprehend which content types and subjects resonate with them. This data forms the bedrock for shaping a content strategy that directly addresses your audience.

Example: A fitness influencer targeting young adults keen on weight loss might carry out audience research to fathom the specific challenges they encounter, their favored workout routines, and nutritional concerns. This information can steer the development of content that tackles those pain points and offers practical guidance.

- **Persona Development**

Create buyer personas or audience profiles that represent distinct segments within your target audience. These personas aid in understanding your audience's motivations, objectives, and behavioral patterns. By constructing personas, you can tailor your content to meet the distinct needs and interests of each segment.

Example: A skincare brand targeting both teenagers and middle-aged adults may formulate two personas: "Teenage Trendsetter" and "Mature Skincare Enthusiast." The content strategy for each persona would differ based on their unique skincare concerns, preferences, and lifestyle factors.

Crafting Engaging Content

- **Content Types and Formats**

Contemplate the types of content that resonate with your audience. This could encompass educational blog posts, entertaining videos, inspiring narratives, or captivating visuals. Opt for content formats that align with your brand and the preferences of your audience.

Example: A travel blogger catering to adventure enthusiasts might generate content in the form of visually stunning photos, immersive travel vlogs, and engaging written stories that spotlight thrilling experiences and dispense practical travel advice.

- **Authenticity and Storytelling**

Authenticity is paramount in forging a sincere connection with your audience. Share personal experiences, anecdotes, and behind-the-scenes glimpses to humanize your brand and make it relatable. Employ storytelling techniques to emotionally engage your audience and create a lasting impact.

Example: A nonprofit organization committed to environmental conservation could disseminate stories of individuals whose lives have been positively impacted by their initiatives. By showcasing real people and their inspiring journeys, the organization can evoke empathy and encourage support from their audience.

- **Consistency and Frequency**

Devise a content calendar to ensure a steady flow of content. Establish a regular posting schedule that aligns with your audience's expectations and the algorithms of the platform. Consistency fosters trust with your audience and keeps them engaged.

Example: A food blogger may commit to publishing a new recipe every Friday and sharing cooking tips and tricks every Tuesday. By upholding a consistent schedule, the blogger becomes a dependable source of culinary inspiration for their audience.

- **Engaging and Interactive Content**

Promote audience participation through interactive content formats such as polls, quizzes, contests, and user-generated content campaigns. Engage in dialogues with your audience by promptly responding to comments and messages.

Example: A beauty brand might organize a contest inviting followers to showcase their favorite makeup looks using the brand's products. This not only boosts engagement but also showcases the creativity and loyalty of their audience.

Measuring Success and Making Improvements

Key Performance Indicators (KPIs):

Identify pertinent KPIs to gauge the effectiveness of your content strategy. These could include metrics like engagement rate, reach, conversions, website traffic, or brand sentiment. Regularly scrutinize these metrics to discern which content resonates most effectively with your audience.

Example: An e-commerce business may monitor conversion rates to gauge the efficacy of their content focused on products. They can assess which content types or specific product features yield the highest conversion rates and fine-tune their strategy accordingly.

A/B Testing

Experiment with diverse content formats, headlines, visuals, and calls to action to ascertain what resonates most with your audience. Employ A/B tests to compare the performance of various variations and refine your content strategy based on these insights.

Example: A software company might test two different headlines for an educational blog post and analyze click-through rates to determine which headline garners higher engagement. This information can guide future headline choices.

Continuous Improvement

Regularly review and evaluate the performance of your content strategy to pinpoint areas for enhancement. Stay abreast of industry trends and evolving audience preferences to ensure your content remains relevant and continues to resonate with your audience over time.

Example: An influencer specializing in personal development may notice shifting trends in their audience's interests and begin incorporating content related to mental health and mindfulness to cater to these evolving needs.

Conclusion

Developing a content strategy that strikes a chord with your audience is pivotal for establishing a robust online presence and fostering meaningful engagement. By comprehending your audience through thorough research, crafting compelling content that aligns with their preferences, and consistently delivering value, you can forge a deep connection with your audience. Remember to maintain authenticity, employ storytelling techniques, and actively engage with your audience. Gauge the success of your content strategy using relevant KPIs, conduct A/B tests, and continuously refine it based on feedback and industry trends. Through ongoing refinement and optimization of your content strategy, you can harness the power of social media to amass followers, unlock benefits, and attain your objectives.

Using Analytics and Metrics to Measure Achievement

To harness the potential of social media effectively, it's vital to assess the results of your efforts. This chapter delves into the significance of employing analytics and metrics to monitor and assess your performance on social media. This empowers you to make informed decisions based on data and fine-tune your strategies for maximum effectiveness.

Establishing Key Performance Indicators (KPIs)

To measure success on social media efficiently, it's imperative to identify and delineate your Key Performance Indicators (KPIs). These are specific metrics aligned with your business objectives, aiding in tracking progress. Common KPIs encompass:

a) Follower Growth: Tracking the rise in your follower count over time serves as an indicator of how effective your content and engagement strategies are.

b) Engagement Rate: Evaluating the level of interaction (likes, comments, shares) your posts receive relative to your follower count offers insights into audience engagement and content quality.

c) Reach and Impressions: Monitoring the number of people who view your posts (reach) and the frequency your posts are displayed (impressions) helps gauge the visibility and potential impact of your content.

d) Click-through Rate (CTR): Analyzing the percentage of users who click on a link or call-to-action in your posts can indicate the effectiveness of your content in driving traffic to your website or other desired destinations.

Social Media Analytics Tools

Various social media analytics tools are available to collect and analyze the necessary data. These tools offer valuable insights into your social media performance, audience demographics, content performance, and more. Some popular tools include:

a) Facebook Insights: Facebook's built-in analytics tool provides a wealth of information about your page's performance, including reach, engagement, and audience demographics.

b) X (Twitter) Analytics: Twitter offers its analytics platform, allowing you to view tweet impressions, engagement metrics, follower growth, and more.

c) Instagram Insights: Instagram's native analytics tool offers valuable data on content performance, follower demographics, and engagement metrics.

d) Google Analytics: While not specific to social media, integrating Google Analytics with your social media platforms can offer a comprehensive view of how social media contributes to website traffic, conversions, and other important metrics.

Case Study: Company X's Social Media Campaign

Let's examine a case study to illustrate how employing analytics and metrics to measure success on social media works in practice.

Company X, an e-commerce brand, launched a social media campaign to promote a new product line. By utilizing Facebook Insights and Google Analytics, they gathered and analyzed the following metrics:

a) Follower Growth: Company X observed a 20% increase in their Facebook followers during the campaign period, indicating a positive response to their content and promotional efforts.

b) Engagement Rate: They noticed a significant rise in post engagement, with likes, comments, and shares increasing by 35% compared to their previous campaigns.

c) Click-through Rate (CTR): By tracking the CTR of their campaign's call-to-action link, Company X discovered that their social media posts drove a 25% increase in traffic to their product pages.

d) Conversion Rate: By integrating Google Analytics, they were able to measure the campaign's impact on sales. They found that the campaign generated a 15% increase in conversions compared to their average conversion rate.

By monitoring these metrics and analyzing the data, Company X gained valuable insights into the success of their social media campaign. They were able to identify the most effective content, optimize their targeting strategies, and allocate their resources more efficiently for future campaigns.

Conclusion

Utilizing analytics and metrics is essential for measuring success on social media. By defining relevant KPIs and leveraging social media analytics tools, you can gain valuable insights into your performance, audience engagement, and the impact of your social media efforts. By making data-driven decisions and continuously optimizing your strategies, you can unlock the full potential of social media and achieve your goals.

Chapter Three

Building a Strong Online Presence

In this chapter, we shall be exploring various methods we can build a compelling and strong online presence in an organically viable manner. We shall break down these guidelines into branded subtopics for effective understanding.

Creating a Compelling and Consistent Brand Identity

Crafting a captivating and uniform brand identity is pivotal in today's digital era, where social media platforms wield substantial influence over brand perception and engagement. A robust brand identity sets you apart from competitors, builds trust with your audience, and nurtures brand loyalty. This chapter will delve into the essential components and tactics for shaping an enticing and consistent brand identity on social media, illustrated by real-world examples from successful brands.

Defining Your Brand Identity

To forge a compelling brand identity, the initial step is to delineate your brand's core values, mission, and distinctive selling proposition. Ponder what distinguishes your brand from others and the image you wish to project to your target audience. This entails comprehending your audience's needs, desires, and preferences. Let's explore how Nike, a globally renowned sports brand, has adeptly shaped its brand identity.

Example: Nike:

Nike's brand identity revolves around the notions of athletic excellence, empowerment, and innovation. They've positioned themselves as a brand that motivates athletes to surpass their limits and "Just Do It." Nike's brand identity is mirrored in their tagline, iconic swoosh logo, and unwavering messaging across their social media channels. By aligning their brand identity with their target audience's aspirations, Nike has cultivated a robust and devoted following.

Consistent Visual Branding

Visual branding assumes a pivotal role in maintaining a coherent brand identity across social media platforms. Consistency in visual elements such as color palette, typography, and imagery bolsters brand recognition and evokes specific emotions. Let's delve into how Coca-Cola has effectively implemented consistent visual branding on social media.

Example: Coca-Cola:

Coca-Cola's brand identity centers on happiness, joy, and togetherness. Their steadfast use of the iconic red and white color scheme, script typography, and images portraying people enjoying moments of connection reinforces their brand identity. Coca-Cola's visual branding is conspicuous across all their social media platforms, establishing a unified and instantly recognizable presence.

Authenticity and Brand Voice

Authenticity constitutes a pivotal facet of an enticing brand identity. Your brand voice should exhibit consistency across all social media channels, reflecting your brand's persona and values. It ought to resonate with your target audience, engaging them in meaningful dialogues. Let's analyze how Wendy's, a fast-food chain, has effectively harnessed an authentic and distinct brand voice on social media.

Example: Wendy's:

Wendy's has garnered substantial attention on social media platforms by embracing a witty, sassy, and occasionally sarcastic brand voice. Their tweets and responses to followers are characterized by humor and playful banter. This brand voice has resonated with their target audience, resulting in heightened engagement and brand loyalty. Wendy's unwavering use of their brand voice across social media platforms has facilitated their prominence in a competitive market.

Storytelling and Emotional Appeal

Proficient storytelling can cultivate an emotional connection between your brand and your audience. By sharing compelling narratives, you can captivate and engage your followers, ultimately reinforcing your brand identity. GoPro, a company recognized for its action cameras, exemplifies the influence of storytelling and emotional appeal on social media.

Example: GoPro:

GoPro's brand identity revolves around adventure, excitement, and capturing extraordinary moments. They harness user-generated content to narrate stories of individuals pushing their boundaries and experiencing thrilling adventures. By disseminating these captivating stories through their social media platforms, GoPro not only inspires their audience but also reaffirms their brand identity as a provider of tools for capturing extraordinary experiences.

Conclusion

Cultivating a compelling and consistent brand identity on social media involves a multifaceted process encompassing the definition of your brand's values, the implementation of uniform visual branding, the adoption of an authentic brand voice, and the utilization of storytelling techniques. Accomplished brands like Nike, Coca-Cola, Wendy's, and GoPro have illustrated how these elements can be effectively employed to establish a robust brand identity, stimulate engagement, and foster loyalty on social media platforms. By implementing these strategies, you can harness the potential of social media to amass followers, unlock advantages, and establish a enduring connection with your audience.

Enhancing Engagement on your Social Media profile through Strategic Optimization

Maximizing engagement with your audience hinges on the effective optimization of your social media profiles. Well-tailored profiles not only capture attention but also convey your brand identity, fostering user interaction. In this chapter, we'll explore key strategies and exemplify best practices for optimizing your social media profiles, drawing inspiration from successful brands.

Ensuring Brand Consistency

Maintaining a unified brand image across your social media profiles is pivotal for establishing a seamless and instantly recognizable presence. Your profile picture, cover photo, and bio should harmonize with your brand's visual identity and messaging. Let's take Starbucks as an example of masterful brand consistency.

Example: Starbucks: Starbucks upholds a consistent brand identity across its social media profiles by featuring its iconic green logo as the profile picture and showcasing high-quality product images as cover photos. Their bio echoes their commitment to top-tier coffee and customer experience. This unwavering branding fosters immediate brand recognition and solidifies their reputation as a trusted coffee provider.

Crafting a Captivating Bio

Crafting a concise yet compelling bio holds the key to capturing the interest of visitors to your social media profiles. Your bio must effectively convey your brand's value proposition, unique selling points, and core messages. Tesla provides an excellent illustration of bio optimization on social media.

Example: Tesla: Tesla's social media profiles boast a concise and impactful bio that encapsulates their brand essence and mission. They underscore their dedication to sustainable energy and innovation, emphasizing their mission to accelerate the global shift toward sustainable transportation. Tesla's bio adeptly communicates their brand's values, resonating with users who share their vision.

Leveraging Keywords and Hashtags

Incorporating pertinent keywords and hashtags within your social media profiles can bolster discoverability and attract users interested in your niche or industry. Conduct thorough keyword research to pinpoint popular terms and phrases relevant to your brand. Employ industry-specific hashtags to engage in conversations and enhance visibility. Sephora demonstrates effective use of keywords and hashtags in profile optimization.

Example: Sephora: Sephora's social media profiles feature pertinent keywords like "beauty," "makeup," and "skincare" in their bios. They also leverage trending hashtags like #beautylover and #makeuptips. By incorporating these keywords and hashtags, Sephora elevates its chances of appearing in search results and reaching users passionate about beauty and skincare products.

Employing a Persuasive Call-to-Action (CTA)

Including a clear and compelling call-to-action in your social media profiles motivates users to take desired actions, such as visiting your website, subscribing to your newsletter, or making a purchase. Amazon serves as an exemplary case of optimizing social media profiles with a clear CTA.

Example: Amazon: Amazon's social media profiles prominently feature a CTA that directs users to their website for shopping. By offering a straightforward and actionable CTA, Amazon encourages users to engage with their brand beyond social media, driving traffic to their online store and boosting conversions.

Conclusion

The optimization of your social media profiles is pivotal for maximizing engagement and attracting your ideal audience. By embracing brand consistency, crafting an engaging bio, integrating relevant keywords and hashtags, and implementing a clear call-to-action, you can optimize your profiles for utmost impact. The successes of brands like Starbucks, Tesla, Sephora, and Amazon illustrate the effectiveness of these strategies in creating captivating and user-friendly social media profiles. Through optimization, you can amplify your brand's visibility, attract a devoted following, and nurture meaningful interactions with your audience

Crafting Compelling and Share-Worthy Social Media Content

To foster audience interaction and broaden your brand's social media reach, it's crucial to produce captivating and shareable content. When your content strikes a chord with your audience, they're more inclined to engage with and disseminate it, magnifying its impact. This chapter will delve into methods for creating engaging and shareable content on social media, illustrated with pertinent examples from successful brands.

The Art of Storytelling

Storytelling serves as a potent tool for seizing your audience's attention and forging a connection. A compelling narrative engages your audience on an emotional level, increasing the likelihood of content sharing. Dove's adept use of storytelling on social media exemplifies this technique.

Example: Dove:

Dove's "Real Beauty" campaign stands as a prime instance of storytelling in action. They share tales that celebrate diversity, challenge conventional beauty norms, and advocate self-acceptance. By disseminating relatable and empowering narratives, Dove fashions content that deeply resonates with their audience, spurring users to share messages of inclusivity and body positivity.

The Visual Allure

Creating visually captivating content is pivotal for seizing attention and stimulating sharing across social media platforms. Striking visuals enable your content to stand out amid the deluge of posts. National Geographic's skillful use of visual appeal to craft engaging and shareable content offers a noteworthy case.

Example: National Geographic:

National Geographic is renowned for its mesmerizing photography and breathtaking visuals. They share enchanting images that showcase the splendor and diversity of the natural world. Through consistently delivering visually alluring content, National Geographic entices their audience to actively engage with their posts and pass them along to others who share an appreciation for our planet's beauty.

Interactivity at Its Core

Interactive content fosters active involvement from your audience, rendering it more engaging and shareable. By involving your audience in the content creation process, you cultivate a sense of ownership, encouraging them to share their experiences. Netflix's utilization of interactive content on social media illustrates this approach.

Example: Netflix:

Netflix frequently crafts interactive content like quizzes, polls, and challenges linked to their shows and movies. By inviting their audience to participate and share their results, Netflix spurs engagement and generates conversations about their content. This interactive approach not only bolsters engagement but also extends the reach of their brand as users share their experiences with others.

Eliciting Emotional Resonance

Content that evokes strong emotions is more likely to be shared on social media. When your content triggers joy, surprise, inspiration, or empathy, it prompts an emotional reaction that compels users to share it. Always showcases the power of emotionally resonant content on social media.

Example: Always:

Always, a feminine hygiene brand, devised the viral "Like a Girl" campaign, which challenged stereotypes and sought to empower young girls. The campaign featured emotional narratives and thought-provoking videos that struck a chord with global audiences. By addressing critical social issues and eliciting profound emotions, Always created content that ignited discussions and garnered widespread sharing.

Conclusion

Producing engaging and shareable content on social media calls for a thoughtful approach that encompasses storytelling, visual allure, interactivity, and emotional resonance. Successful brands like Dove, National Geographic, Netflix, and Always exemplify how these strategies can be adeptly harnessed to shape content that captures audiences' attention and encourages sharing. By implementing these tactics, you can elevate engagement, amplify your brand's reach, and nurture meaningful connections with your social media audience.

Unleashing the Potential of Visuals: Pictures, Videos, and Infographics.

The art of seizing your audience's attention is paramount. Visual content, encompassing images, videos, and infographics, stands as a potent means of conveying information, stirring emotions, and kindling engagement. This chapter delves into the significance of visuals in the realm of social media and offers glimpses of triumphs by brands that have adeptly harnessed their power.

Images

Images constitute a fundamental facet of social media content, swiftly seizing users' attention amidst their feeds. They serve to convey messages, flaunt products, and elicit emotions. Airbnb provides an enlightening case study in the effective use of images on social media.

Example: Airbnb:

Airbnb frequently shares awe-inspiring images of distinctive lodgings and travel destinations across their social media profiles. These images ensnare users' focus, beckoning them to explore further. By showcasing high-quality visuals that illuminate the experiences their platform offers, Airbnb adeptly conveys their brand's essence, inspiring users to interact with their content and disseminate it among their networks.

Videos

Videos have surged in popularity on social media, affording brands the opportunity to narrate stories, showcase products, and engage their audience in a dynamic manner. GoPro furnishes a compelling example of leveraging video content to forge a connection with their audience.

Example: GoPro:

GoPro, recognized for its action cameras, crafts exhilarating video content that spotlights extreme sports, adventures, and awe-inspiring escapades. Their videos immerse viewers in the action, evoking exhilaration and a sense of wonder. By disseminating these riveting videos on social media, GoPro stimulates engagement, inspires user-generated content, and amplifies brand recognition.

Infographics

Infographics fuse visual elements with succinct text to present intricate information in an aesthetically pleasing and readily digestible format. They possess high shareability and excel in conveying data, statistics, and step-by-step processes. HubSpot provides an illustrative instance of infographics within their social media strategy.

Example: HubSpot:

HubSpot routinely forges infographics to communicate valuable marketing and sales insights via their social media platforms. Their infographics proficiently portray data and statistics in a visually captivating fashion, rendering intricate information more accessible. By disseminating these infographics, HubSpot not only imparts value to their audience but also spurs engagement, shares, and references as a credible source of information.

Visual Cohesion

Sustaining visual uniformity across your social media profiles stands as a linchpin for brand recognition and the cultivation of a coherent visual identity. The consistent application of colors, fonts, and visual elements bolsters your brand's image. Coca-Cola offers a compelling illustration of visual consistency in the realm of social media.

Example: Coca-Cola:

Coca-Cola perennially infuses their hallmark red hue and iconic logo into their visual content across social media. Whether they disseminate images, videos, or infographics, their content mirrors their brand's visual identity. This steadfastness fortifies their brand recognition and enables users to link their content unmistakably with Coca-Cola.

Conclusion

Visual content assumes a pivotal role in captivating attention, transmitting messages, and igniting engagement across social media. Accomplished brands like Airbnb, GoPro, HubSpot, and Coca-Cola have adroitly harnessed the potency of visuals, employing images, videos, and infographics. Through the adept use of these visual elements, brands can wield a commanding influence, evoke emotions, and motivate users to engage with and distribute their content. The inclusion of visually appealing and harmonious elements within your social media strategy can amplify your brand's visibility, augment engagement, and nurture profound connections with your audience.

Utilizing User-Generated Content and Collaborations with Influencers

Harnessing the potential of user-generated content (UGC) and forming partnerships with influencers have emerged as potent strategies for brands seeking to elevate their presence and engage their social media audience. This chapter delves into the advantages of leveraging UGC and influencer collaborations, while showcasing instances of brands that have adeptly implemented these approaches.

User-Generated Content (UGC)

UGC encompasses any content type—be it images, videos, reviews, testimonials—generated by consumers or users of a brand's products or services. UGC injects authenticity, credibility, and social validation into your social media presence. Consider Starbucks as an example of an entity capitalizing on UGC.

Example: Starbucks:

Starbucks actively encourages its patrons to share their Starbucks experiences on social media using the hashtag #Starbucks. They curate and feature UGC that showcases their offerings, from customers enjoying their favorite Starbucks concoctions to artistic latte designs. By spotlighting UGC, Starbucks not only engages its audience but also fosters a sense of community, motivating others to share their Starbucks moments, thereby sparking a ripple effect of UGC across social media platforms.

Influencer Collaborations

Influencer collaborations involve partnerships with individuals boasting substantial followings and sway in the realm of social media. These influencers can serve as amplifiers for your brand's messaging, extending its reach to a broader audience and driving engagement. The case of Adidas offers insight into the successful application of influencer partnerships.

Example: Adidas:

Adidas frequently teams up with athletes, celebrities, and social media influencers to endorse their products and campaigns. They opt for influencers whose values and target audience align with their brand. For instance, Adidas collaborated with fitness influencer Kayla Itsines to promote their workout attire and training programs. By harnessing the expansive reach and influence of such partnerships, Adidas expands its brand's sphere of influence, bolsters its credibility, and spurs user engagement.

Co-Creation Endeavors

Co-creation campaigns entail collaborative content creation endeavors involving users or influencers. This approach fosters a sense of camaraderie, community, and participation. An exemplar of this strategy can be witnessed in GoPro's practices.

Example: GoPro:

GoPro orchestrates diverse co-creation campaigns, inviting their user base to submit their most exhilarating videos captured with GoPro cameras. They subsequently showcase the chosen user-generated videos on their social media platforms, giving due credit to the creators. This methodology not only stimulates engagement from their audience but also underscores the capabilities of their products, inspiring others to craft and share their content utilizing GoPro cameras.

Social Media Challenges

Social media challenges have gained immense traction as a means to engage users and motivate them to conceive and disseminate content aligned with a particular theme or activity. These challenges can rapidly become viral sensations, drawing substantial participation and brand exposure. The ALS Ice Bucket Challenge serves as a paradigmatic illustration of this phenomenon.

Example: ALS Ice Bucket Challenge:

The ALS Ice Bucket Challenge encompassed a social media campaign where participants recorded themselves dousing their heads with ice-cold water, all in the name of raising awareness and funds for amyotrophic lateral sclerosis (ALS). The challenge swiftly went viral, with millions sharing their videos across social media platforms. The campaign masterfully leveraged UGC, elicited user involvement on a massive scale, ultimately resulting in widespread awareness and generous donations for ALS research.

Conclusion

Harnessing user-generated content and forging influencer collaborations on social media can wield a substantial impact on your brand's visibility, engagement, and reach. Brands such as Starbucks, Adidas, GoPro, and iconic campaigns like the ALS Ice Bucket Challenge exemplify the adept execution of these strategies. By weaving UGC into your social media fabric, collaborating with influencers, orchestrating co-creation initiatives, and propelling social media challenges, brands can tap into the compelling forces of user participation, authenticity, and social influence. In doing so, they can cultivate meaningful bonds with their audience and ignite pervasive engagement across social media platforms.

Chapter Four

Growing Your Follower Base

Employing strategies to garner organic social media followers can significantly contribute to the growth and prosperity of your social media presence. Unlike paid followers, organic followers are individuals who authentically engage with your content, share it organically, and transform into steadfast advocates for your brand. Below are some proficient strategies to captivate organic social media followers:

Craft High-Quality and Captivating Content

The creation of compelling and valuable content stands as a cornerstone in attracting and retaining organic followers. Focus on producing content that informs, entertains, inspires, or educates, tailored to your specific niche and target audience. Employ a diverse array of formats, including videos, images, infographics, and written posts, to cater to varied preferences. For example, if your domain is a fitness blog, you can craft workout videos, instructional recipes, and motivational posts to actively engage your audience.

Understand Your Target Audience

Acquiring an in-depth understanding of your target audience proves pivotal in luring organic followers who genuinely resonate with your content. Conduct comprehensive research to discern their demographics, interests, pain points, and preferences. By tailoring your content to meet their needs, you can draw followers genuinely intrigued by what you offer. For instance, if your audience comprises young professionals interested in personal finance, you can generate content centered on budgeting tips, investment strategies, and career advancement insights.

Harness Hashtags Effectively

Hashtags wield substantial influence in extending your reach and beckoning organic followers. Delve into research to identify pertinent and trending hashtags within your niche, and seamlessly integrate them into your posts. This enhances the visibility of your content by making it discoverable in hashtag searches. Nonetheless, it is paramount to strike a balance and avoid excessive hashtag use, which can render your posts appear spammy. While platforms like Instagram and Twitter permit multiple hashtags, it's prudent to opt for a select few on platforms like Facebook.

Foster Engagement with Your Audience

Active engagement with your audience forms the bedrock of relationship-building and the attraction of organic followers. Timely and thoughtful responses to comments, messages, and mentions demonstrate your genuine interest. Encourage dialogues by posing questions, seeking opinions, and prompting followers to share their experiences. By nurturing a sense of community and making your audience feel valued, you pave the way for the cultivation of loyal followers who actively engage with your content and advocate for it.

Collaborate with Influencers and Experts in Your Field

Collaborating with influencers and experts within your niche can widen your reach and magnetize organic followers. When influencers or authorities share your content or endorse your brand, their followers are more inclined to trust and follow you. Seek out influencers whose values align with your brand and whose followers align with your target audience. Collaboration possibilities abound, ranging from guest blog contributions to joint social media initiatives or influencer takeovers.

Cross-Promote Across Multiple Platforms

Promoting your social media accounts on other platforms can beckon organic followers who are already engaged with your brand elsewhere. For instance, if you maintain a popular blog, incorporate social media buttons on your website to beckon readers to follow you on social platforms. Similarly, advocate for your social media accounts within your email newsletters, YouTube videos, or podcast episodes, if applicable. This practice of cross-promotion leverages your pre-existing audience and encourages them to connect with you on diverse social media platforms.

In summary, attracting organic social media followers necessitates the consistent implementation of a multifaceted strategy encompassing superior content, an intimate understanding of your audience, astute hashtag utilization, active engagement, strategic collaborations, and cross-platform promotion. By adhering to these tactics, you can expand your reach, cultivate a devoted follower base, and nurture profound connections with your audience.

Mastering the Art of Hashtags

Hashtags have risen to prominence as a defining feature on social media platforms, offering users a means to categorize content and engage in broader conversations. When wielded effectively, hashtags possess the power to augment visibility, stimulate engagement, and magnetize a precisely targeted audience. This article will delve into the art of using hashtags skillfully on social media, bolstered by illustrative examples to underscore their impact.

Meticulous Hashtag Research

Prior to integrating hashtags into your social media posts, it's imperative to embark on comprehensive research to pinpoint the most apt ones. Consider these steps:

a) Scrutinize your content: Identify the fundamental topics, keywords, and themes encapsulated in your post.

b) Probe into popular hashtags: Explore platforms like Instagram, Twitter, and TikTok to unearth trending and popular hashtags aligned with your content.

c) Embrace niche hashtags: In tandem with popular hashtags, unearth specialized or industry-specific hashtags that cater to your target audience and bestow a competitive edge amidst the clamor.

Example: Suppose you're a fitness influencer disseminating workout regimens. Relevant hashtags may encompass #FitLife, #FitnessMotivation, or #WorkoutInspiration. Meanwhile, niche hashtags such as #YogaLovers or #CrossFitCommunity can ensnare a more specialized audience.

Precision and Brevity

To extract the utmost potential from hashtags, precision and brevity should be your guiding principles. Concentrate on deploying pertinent keywords that faithfully represent your content. Steer clear of protracted, intricate hashtags that might bewilder or dissuade user engagement.

Example: Instead of adopting an overarching hashtag like #Food, a gastronomy blogger might prefer precision, utilizing more specific hashtags like #VeganRecipes or #FoodPhotographyTips to captivate an audience keen on those subjects.

Harness Trending Hashtags

Tapping into prevailing and trending hashtags can wield substantial influence, catapulting your content's visibility and engagement to new heights. Stay attuned to trending topics, events, holidays, or viral challenges that seamlessly align with your brand or content.

Example: On momentous occasions such as the Olympics or the Super Bowl, brands often incorporate pertinent hashtags like #Tokyo2020 or #SuperBowlLV to partake in the discourse and reach an expansive audience.

Hashtags on Reels

When it comes to using hashtags on Reels, the effectiveness of using a large number of hashtags versus a limited number depends on various factors. However, generally speaking, it's important to focus on using relevant and popular hashtags rather than simply using a large quantity of hashtags. Let us use Facebook Reels as a case study.

If you use hashtags that have millions of existing tags, such as popular and widely-used hashtags, your content might get lost among the vast number of posts using the same hashtag. In this case, it can be challenging to stand out and attract views unless your content is exceptionally unique or compelling.

On the other hand, if you use hashtags in a subject that has limited tags, there might be fewer posts competing for attention under those hashtags. This could potentially increase the visibility of your content among the limited pool of posts using those hashtags. However, it's important to note that if the subject has limited tags, it might also indicate a smaller audience or less interest in that particular topic.

To maximize the views and engagement on your Facebook Reels, it's generally recommended to follow these guidelines:

1. Use relevant hashtags: Choose hashtags that are directly related to the content of your Reel. This will help your content reach users who are specifically interested in that subject matter.

2. Mix popular and niche hashtags: Combine popular hashtags that have a larger reach with niche hashtags that are more targeted to your specific content. This way, you can potentially tap into broader audiences while still reaching people who are interested in your specific niche.

3. Be specific and creative: Consider using unique or creative hashtags that are specific to your content. This can help distinguish your Reels from others and attract viewers who are looking for something fresh and original.

4. Research and analyze: Take the time to research which hashtags are popular and trending within your niche. You can also analyze the performance of your previous Reels to identify which hashtags have generated more views and engagement. This data can guide your hashtag strategy and help you make informed decisions.

Remember, while hashtags can increase the visibility of your Facebook Reels, the quality and relevance of your content ultimately play a significant role in attracting views and engagement.

Forge Branded Hashtags

Crafting distinct branded hashtags can fortify your brand's identity and galvanize user-generated content. Branded hashtags serve as rallying points for your community and simplify the tracking and interaction with user-generated content connected to your brand.

Example: Coca-Cola's #ShareACoke initiative encouraged consumers to share images of personalized Coke bottles on social media, catalyzing a viral phenomenon and increasing brand visibility.

Tailor to Platforms-Specific Hashtags

Distinct social media platforms harbor their unique hashtag cultures and inclinations. Adapt your hashtag strategy to each platform by grasping the subtleties and inclinations of its user base.

Example: Instagram users frequently incorporate location-specific hashtags like #NYCFoodie or #LAStyle to appeal to local audiences, while Twitter's landscape is marked by the use of hashtags to partake in real-time conversations and trending topics.

Vigilant Monitoring and Engagement

Hashtags function as conduits to connect with your audience. Vigilantly monitor the hashtags you employ and interact with users who engage with your content under those hashtags. Respond to comments, acknowledge user-generated content, and kindle dialogues surrounding your brand.

Example: Starbucks encourages patrons to share their Starbucks encounters via the hashtag #Starbucks on social media. The company actively fosters engagement by liking, resharing, and responding to posts featuring the hashtag.

Conclusion

The adept utilization of hashtags on social media can amplify your content's reach, galvanize engagement, and facilitate a connection with your intended audience. By embarking on meticulous research, wielding specific and concise hashtags, capitalizing on trends, crafting branded hashtags, tailoring to platform-specific etiquettes, and actively engaging with users, you can harness the full potential of hashtags to elevate your social media presence and realize your marketing goals

Interacting with your Followers through Comments, Likes, and Shares

Interacting with your audience through comments, likes, and shares on social media plays a pivotal role in building a robust online presence and fostering genuine connections with your followers. By actively joining discussions, acknowledging user-generated content, and encouraging interaction, you can cultivate a lively and engaged community around your brand or personal profile. Below are some effective approaches and instances of how to engage with your social media audience:

Responding to comments: Dedicate time to read and reply to comments on your social media posts. Whether it involves answering queries, offering more information, or expressing gratitude, responding to comments demonstrates your appreciation for your audience's input and encourages further engagement. For instance, if you're a fashion influencer and someone inquires about the clothing brand you're wearing in a post, you can respond with the brand name and share your thoughts on the product's quality.

Asking questions: Pose thought-provoking questions in your social media captions or posts to prompt your audience to share their thoughts and experiences. This stimulates conversation and provides valuable insights into your followers' interests and preferences. For example, if you run a food blog, you could inquire about your audience's favorite cuisine or recipe, encouraging them to engage by leaving comments and sharing their recommendations.

Liking and reacting to comments: Express gratitude for your audience's contributions by liking and reacting to their comments. This simple gesture acknowledges their engagement and motivates them to continue interacting with your content. Additionally, liking comments can enhance visibility, as other users may notice the interaction and be more inclined to join the conversation. For instance, if you're a travel blogger and someone expresses excitement about visiting a particular destination in a comment, you can like their comment to show your enthusiasm and encourage further engagement.

Sharing user-generated content: Recognize and highlight your audience's creativity and loyalty by sharing their content on your own social media platforms. This could involve reposting their photos, featuring their testimonials, or showcasing their success stories. By doing so, you not only strengthen your relationship with your followers but also inspire others to engage and contribute their own content. For example, a fitness brand could create a dedicated hashtag for users to share their workout progress and then select and repost some of the best submissions, giving credit to the original creators.

Running contests and giveaways: Organize contests or giveaways that require audience participation, such as sharing, commenting, or tagging friends. This not only generates excitement but also boosts engagement and expands your reach as participants spread the word about your content or brand. For instance, a beauty brand could ask followers to share their favorite makeup looks using a specific hashtag and randomly select a winner to receive a product bundle.

Remember, the key to engaging with your audience through comments, likes, and shares on social media lies in prioritizing authenticity, responsiveness, and meaningful interactions. By actively participating and nurturing your online community, you can cultivate a loyal following and establish a strong brand presence in the digital landscape

Cross-Promotion and Partnership with Fellow Accounts

Cross-promotion and partnerships with fellow accounts have gained popularity among individuals, brands, and influencers as effective strategies to widen their audience, interact with fresh followers, and enhance their overall presence on social platforms. By teaming up with other accounts, users can access established communities and make use of the existing followers and engagement of their partners. This mutually advantageous approach enables both parties to gain exposure and create a win-win scenario.

One prevalent form of cross-promotion is the "shoutout," where one account publicly acknowledges or endorses another. For example, a fashion blogger might give a shoutout to a makeup artist, showcasing their work and encouraging their followers to explore the artist's profile. This can be accomplished through posts, stories, or dedicated content featuring the collaborator's material.

Another popular collaboration method involves hosting joint contests or giveaways. This entails partnering with another account to offer a shared prize or a bundle of products/services. By pooling their resources, both accounts can attract a larger audience and generate more engagement. For instance, an athletic apparel brand might collaborate with a fitness influencer to host a giveaway, where participants must follow both accounts and tag friends for a chance to win.

Influencer takeovers represent another effective collaboration approach. This involves temporarily granting another user access to your social media account to create and share content. This strategy enables both parties to benefit from each other's followers and expertise. For example, a travel blogger might collaborate with a food blogger, allowing the food blogger to take over the travel blogger's Instagram account for a day and share their culinary experiences during their journeys.

Collaborations can also involve content exchanges or guest appearances. For instance, a YouTuber might invite another popular YouTuber to feature in their video, offering their audience exposure to the guest's content and vice versa. Similarly, brands can partner with relevant influencers or content creators to produce sponsored content or product reviews, delivering valuable exposure to their target audience.

Social media platforms themselves actively promote cross-promotion and collaboration. For instance, Instagram introduced the "Paid Partnership" feature, enabling users to tag other accounts when collaborating or promoting a sponsored product. This feature enhances transparency and credibility while acknowledging the collaborating account.

A noteworthy example of a successful cross-promotion is the partnership between GoPro and Red Bull. Both brands share a common target audience interested in extreme sports and adventure. They collaborated to create captivating content featuring Red Bull athletes using GoPro cameras, showcasing thrilling experiences from unique perspectives. This collaboration allowed both brands to tap into each other's engaged communities and leverage the synergy between their products.

In conclusion, cross-promotion and collaborations with other social media accounts serve as potent strategies for expanding reach, engaging with new audiences, and strengthening one's presence on social media. Shoutouts, joint contests, influencer takeovers, content exchanges, and guest appearances are all effective ways to collaborate. By teaming up with relevant accounts and leveraging each other's followers and engagement, individuals, brands, and influencers can achieve mutual benefits and make a more significant impact in the social media landscape

Running Focused Advertising Campaigns

Creating focused advertising campaigns entails tailoring your marketing endeavors to connect with specific demographics, interests, and behaviors of your intended audience. By directing your ads towards those most likely to be interested in your products or services, you can enhance campaign effectiveness and achieve a higher return on investment. Here are essential steps and illustrations for executing targeted advertising campaigns:

Identify your target audience: Begin by clearly defining the characteristics of your ideal customers, considering factors like age, gender, location, income, occupation, and interests. For example, if you're promoting a fitness app, your target audience might be health-conscious urban individuals aged 25-40.

Employ data and analytics: Use data and analytics tools to gain insights into your audience's preferences, behaviors, and online activities. This data can come from sources like website analytics, social media, customer surveys, and third-party data providers. For instance, Facebook Audience Insights helps understand the demographics and interests of your Facebook followers.

Choose suitable advertising channels: Select advertising channels that align with your target audience's preferences and behaviors. This may include social media (e.g., Facebook, Instagram), search engine advertising (e.g., Google Ads), display networks, or even traditional media (e.g., TV, radio). For a younger audience, platforms like TikTok or Snapchat may yield success.

Craft personalized messages: Customize your ad messages to resonate with your target audience's needs, interests, and aspirations. For instance, if you're promoting a luxury travel experience, your ads should evoke exclusivity and adventure appealing to affluent travelers.

Implement audience segmentation: Divide your target audience into smaller segments based on specific criteria to create more personalized and relevant ads. For example, a clothing retailer might segment by gender, age, and style preferences to deliver targeted ads for different customer groups.

Utilize remarketing techniques: Use remarketing campaigns to re-engage users who previously interacted with your brand but didn't convert. Show tailored ads across various platforms to boost brand recall and encourage revisits or purchases. For instance, show ads for items left in a cart on other websites visited by the user.

Conduct A/B testing and optimization: Continuously monitor and improve campaign performance. Run A/B tests to compare ad variations, targeting options, or landing pages, and use data to refine your strategies.

A prime example of successful targeted advertising is Amazon's personalized recommendations. Analyzing customer behavior and purchase history, Amazon delivers highly targeted product recommendations to individual users, enhancing customer engagement and sales.

In summary, effective targeted advertising involves understanding your audience, using data and analytics, selecting appropriate channels, tailoring messages, segmenting audiences, employing remarketing, and optimizing campaigns. By applying these strategies and learning from successful cases like Amazon's personalized recommendations, you can maximize your advertising impact and achieve superior results.

Chapter Five

Leveraging the Benefits of Social Media

In an era where platforms like Facebook, Instagram, Twitter, and LinkedIn boast billions of active users, businesses find themselves presented with unparalleled opportunities to connect, interact, and nurture relationships with their clientele through social media. This chapter delves into effective approaches for enhancing customer engagement and loyalty on social platforms, accompanied by relevant instances.

Maintaining a Unified Brand Voice and Messaging

Consistency in brand voice and messaging across various social media channels is essential for establishing a robust rapport with customers. By steadfastly upholding their brand values, companies can forge an authentic and easily recognizable presence. A notable case in point is Wendy's, a fast-food chain, which has garnered a devoted Twitter following by adopting a witty and cheeky tone in their customer interactions. This unwavering brand voice has enabled Wendy's to stand out and amass a dedicated social media following.

Swift and Engaging Responses

Customers today anticipate swift responses when they reach out to businesses on social media. Timely addressing of queries, comments, and complaints showcases a commitment to customer satisfaction. A prominent example lies within the airline industry, where companies like KLM and Southwest

Airlines shine in delivering responsive customer service on social platforms. These airlines have dedicated teams vigilantly monitoring their social media accounts, promptly addressing customer inquiries and resolving issues, which has translated into heightened customer contentment and loyalty.

Tailored Personal Interaction

Customizing interactions to suit individual customers can significantly enhance engagement and foster loyalty. Social media platforms offer businesses ample opportunities to collect customer data and insights, facilitating personalized interaction. Netflix stands as a prime illustration of leveraging personalization on social media. Through the analysis of viewer preferences and behavior, Netflix recommends personalized content on social platforms, thereby engaging customers on a one-to-one level and fortifying loyalty.

User-Generated Content and Competitions

Encouraging users to create content related to a brand and organizing competitions can generate excitement, amplify engagement, and bolster customer loyalty. GoPro, a producer of action cameras, has effectively harnessed user-generated content to captivate its audience. By inspiring customers to share their thrilling content captured with GoPro cameras, the company has constructed a vibrant community and bolstered brand loyalty.

Collaborations with Influencers

Collaborating with social media influencers who resonate with a brand's values and target audience can significantly amplify engagement and loyalty. Influencers possess a dedicated following and can adeptly promote products or services via their social media channels. Gymshark, a fitness apparel brand, has adeptly leveraged influencer partnerships to engage customers on social media. Through alliances with fitness influencers, Gymshark has expanded its reach, gained credibility, and cultivated a devoted customer base.

Exclusive Offers and Rewards

Extending exclusive offers, discounts, and rewards to social media followers can incentivize engagement and foster loyalty. Starbucks, for instance, runs promotions exclusively for their social media followers, such as offering discounted drinks or special menu items. This strategy not only encourages customers to follow and engage with the brand but also creates a sense of exclusivity and appreciation, resulting in heightened loyalty.

Conclusion

Incorporating effective strategies for improving customer engagement and loyalty on social media remains paramount for businesses in the contemporary digital landscape. By upholding a consistent brand voice, responding promptly to customers, personalizing interactions, capitalizing on user-generated content and influencers, and providing exclusive offers, businesses can forge meaningful connections with their customers, nurture loyalty, and chart a course for long-term success. These strategies, together with the examples provided, underscore the potential of social media platforms as potent tools for customer engagement and loyalty.

Generating Leads and Driving Website Traffic

To generate leads and boost website traffic, it is vital to create a potent strategy that enhances your online visibility and engages your desired audience. Here are some crucial actions to help you attain your objectives:

Determine your target audience: It's pivotal to comprehend your ideal audience to craft pertinent and captivating content. Identify the demographics, interests, and online behavior of your potential customers to customize your messaging accordingly.

Select the appropriate social media platforms: Not all social media platforms are equally effective for every business. Conduct research to pinpoint the platforms where your target audience is most active. Concentrate your efforts on these platforms to optimize your reach and engagement.

Enhance your social media profiles: Ensure that your social media profiles are comprehensive, professional, and uniform across platforms. Utilize high-quality visuals, compelling descriptions, and pertinent keywords to captivate and maintain your audience's attention.

Produce valuable and shareable content: Develop a content strategy that delivers value to your audience. Share informative blog posts, captivating videos, eye-catching images, and interactive infographics. Aim to educate, entertain, or inspire your audience, making your content shareable and broadening its reach.

Utilize visual content: Visual content is more likely to attract attention and drive engagement on social media. Integrate visual elements such as images, videos, infographics, and GIFs into your posts to make them more appealing and shareable.

Employ hashtags strategically: Conduct research and employ pertinent hashtags in your social media posts to enhance discoverability. Hashtags facilitate the discovery of your content by users interested in specific topics. However, avoid excessive use; opt for a few well-researched and targeted hashtags rather than a lengthy list of generic ones.

Engage with your audience: Social media is a two-way street, so actively interact with your audience. Respond to comments, address queries, acknowledge feedback, and participate in conversations. Cultivating relationships with your audience builds trust and encourages them to visit your website.

Execute targeted advertising campaigns: Social media platforms offer robust advertising options that enable you to reach a specific audience based on demographics, interests, and behaviors. Invest in targeted ad campaigns to enhance visibility, drive traffic, and generate leads for your website.

Harness influencers and partnerships: Collaborate with influencers or businesses in your industry to extend your reach. Influencers can promote your content to their engaged audience, directing traffic to your website and generating leads.

Monitor and analyze outcomes: Regularly track your social media endeavors using analytics tools. Monitor key metrics such as engagement, reach, click-through rates, and conversions. Analyzing data helps you discern what's effective and what requires improvement, allowing you to refine your strategy over time.

Remember, consistency, high-quality content, and authentic engagement are fundamental for generating leads and increasing website traffic via social media. By implementing these steps and continually optimizing your approach, you can maximize your social media presence and achieve your marketing goals

Exploring E-Commerce Opportunities

Investigating the potential of e-commerce through social media can transform the game for businesses seeking to expand their online footprint and reach a broader audience. With a well-devised approach, companies can harness social media platforms to boost sales, enhance brand visibility, and foster customer engagement. Below are some crucial aspects to consider when exploring e-commerce avenues on social media:

Establish a social media shop: Numerous social media platforms, including Facebook and Instagram, offer integrated e-commerce capabilities that enable businesses to showcase and sell their products directly on their profiles. By setting up a social media shop, you can offer a seamless shopping experience without requiring users to leave the platform.

Utilize shoppable posts and tags: Shoppable posts and tags allow businesses to label their products in social media posts, simplifying the purchasing process for users. For example, Instagram's Shopping feature enables businesses to tag products in their posts, providing a direct link to the product page on their website.

Execute targeted ad campaigns: Social media platforms provide robust advertising tools that empower businesses to create highly focused ad campaigns. You can leverage these features to reach specific audiences based on demographics, interests, and behaviors. By directing your ads to relevant audiences, you can boost traffic to your e-commerce website and drive sales.

Collaborate with influencers: Influencer marketing is a potent tool for e-commerce entities. Partnering with influencers in your industry can help you access their engaged audience, establish trust, and increase sales. Influencers can generate sponsored content showcasing your products, offer discount codes or affiliate links, and share their personal experiences with your brand.

Harness user-generated content: Encourage your customers to produce and share content featuring your products. User-generated content (UGC) adds authenticity to your brand and serves as social proof, which can enhance conversions. You can organize contests or campaigns that incentivize users to create UGC and share it on social media.

Extend exclusive promotions and discounts: Social media platforms provide an ideal platform to offer exclusive promotions and discounts to your followers. Create time-limited offers, flash sales, or unique discount codes specifically for your social media audience. This can create a sense of urgency and drive traffic to your e-commerce website.

Provide exceptional customer service: Social media platforms serve as a direct communication channel between businesses and customers. Respond promptly to customer inquiries, address concerns, and offer support. By delivering outstanding customer service, you can build trust, reinforce customer relationships, and ultimately drive repeat purchases.

Analyze data and optimize: Utilize social media analytics tools to monitor and assess the performance of your e-commerce initiatives. Keep an eye on metrics like engagement, click-through rates, conversions, and revenue generated. This data will help you identify successful strategies and areas that require improvement, enabling you to optimize your approach accordingly.

A successful instance of e-commerce opportunities on social media is the emergence of "social commerce" in China. Platforms like WeChat and Xiaohongshu have integrated e-commerce functions, allowing users to seamlessly discover, share, and purchase products within the app. This has resulted in a substantial increase in e-commerce transactions through social media platforms in China.

In summary, exploring e-commerce potential on social media necessitates a carefully planned strategy that includes social media shops, shoppable posts, targeted advertising, influencer collaborations, user-generated content, exclusive promotions, and exceptional customer service. By effectively leveraging these opportunities, businesses can tap into the vast potential of social media to drive online sales and expand their e-commerce presence.

Chapter Six

Navigating Challenges and Ensuring Success

Whether you're an individual, a business, or an organization, navigating the challenges and ensuring success on social media can be a daunting task. However, with careful planning, strategy, and a few key considerations, you can effectively utilize social media to your advantage. In this chapter, we discuss some essential tips to help you navigate challenges and achieve success on social media

Dealing with negative comments and online trolls

In the realm of social media, negative comments and online trolls are unfortunate realities that many individuals, businesses, and organizations have to face. These can be challenging to handle, but with the right approach, you can effectively manage and minimize their impact. Here are some strategies for dealing with negative comments and online trolls on social media:

1. **Stay Calm and Don't Engage Emotionally**: When encountering negative comments or trolls, it's important to remain calm and composed. Responding with anger or defensiveness can escalate the situation and potentially harm your reputation. Take a deep breath, step away if needed, and approach the situation with a level head.

2. **Assess the Validity of the Comment:** Not all negative comments are baseless or unfounded. Evaluate the feedback objectively to determine if there is any merit to it. Constructive

criticism, even if delivered in a negative tone, can provide valuable insights for improvement. Separate genuine concerns from trolling behavior.

3. Consider Ignoring or Deleting: Sometimes, it is best to ignore negative comments or trolls, especially if they are irrelevant, offensive, or have no constructive value. Engaging with trolls often gives them the attention they seek, which can encourage further negative behavior. Deleting or hiding inappropriate comments is also an option to maintain a positive environment on your social media platforms.

4. Respond with Empathy and Professionalism: If the comment warrants a response, choose your words carefully. Responding with empathy and professionalism can defuse tension and demonstrate your commitment to addressing concerns. Acknowledge the person's perspective, offer assistance, and provide factual information if needed. Avoid getting into arguments or personal attacks.

5. Take Conversations Offline: In some cases, it may be more productive to take the conversation offline. Offer the individual the opportunity to discuss the matter privately through direct messages, email, or other appropriate channels. This allows for a more in-depth discussion and can help resolve the issue without further public escalation.

6. Engage Your Community: Your loyal followers and supporters can be powerful allies in dealing with negative comments and trolls. Encourage your community to respond positively and counteract negativity with their own comments. Their support can drown out the negative voices and create a more balanced discussion.

7. Use Humor or Redirect the Conversation: Humor can be an effective tool to diffuse tension and redirect the conversation. Responding to trolls with a lighthearted or witty comment can sometimes disarm them and discourage further negative behavior. Alternatively, you can shift the focus of the conversation to a more positive or productive topic.

8. Document and Report Harassment: If you encounter online harassment or abusive behavior, it's important to document the instances and report them to the appropriate social media platform. Most platforms have mechanisms in place to report harassment, and taking action against repeat offenders can help create a safer online environment.

9. Seek Support and Guidance: Dealing with negative comments and trolls can be emotionally draining. Reach out to friends, colleagues, or professionals for support and guidance. They can provide valuable perspectives, advice, and help you **navigate through challenging situations.**

10. Focus on the Positive: It is easy to get caught up in negativity, but remember to focus on the positive aspects of social media. Celebrate your loyal followers, engage with constructive conversations, and highlight the positive impact you're making. By maintaining a positive mindset, you can minimize the impact of negative comments and trolls.

Remember, it's impossible to please everyone on social media, and encountering negative comments or trolls is often unavoidable. However, by adopting a calm and professional approach, leveraging community support, and prioritizing constructive engagement, you can effectively manage these challenges and maintain a positive online presence.

Managing Time and Resources Effectively

Social media can be a powerful tool for individuals and businesses, but it can also be a time-consuming and resource-intensive endeavor. To make the most of your time and resources on social media, it's essential to have a well-defined strategy and efficient practices in place. Here are some tips for managing time and resources effectively on social media:

1. **Set Clear Goals and Prioritize**: Start by setting clear goals for your social media efforts. Determine what you want to achieve, whether it's increasing brand awareness, driving website traffic, generating leads, or building customer relationships. Once you have your goals defined, prioritize your activities based on their importance and impact.

2. **Choose the Right Platforms**: This cannot be overemphasized. We have dealt with this aspect earlier but it needs to be re-emphasized. Not all social media platforms will be equally beneficial for your objectives. Identify the platforms where your target audience is most active and focus your efforts there. Trying to maintain a presence on every platform can spread your resources thin and lead to inefficiencies.

3. **Plan and Schedule Content**: Develop a content calendar to plan and schedule your social media content in advance. This allows you to maintain a consistent posting schedule and frees up time for other activities. Use social media management tools like Hootsuite or Buffer to schedule and automate posts across multiple platforms.

4. **Repurpose and Recycle Content**: Don't feel the need to create entirely new content for every social media post.

Repurpose and recycle existing content to maximize its reach and impact. For example, turn a blog post into a series of social media updates, or convert a video into shorter clips or GIFs.

5. **Automate Routine Tasks**: Take advantage of automation tools to streamline routine tasks. Set up automatic notifications for mentions, messages, and comments to ensure timely responses without constantly monitoring social media platforms. Use chatbots to handle common inquiries and provide basic customer support.

6. **Engage with Efficiency**: Engaging with your audience is crucial for building relationships and fostering loyalty. However, it's important to do it efficiently. Set aside specific time slots dedicated to responding to comments, messages, and mentions. Use saved replies or templates for frequently asked questions to save time while still providing personalized responses.

7. **Monitor Analytics and Adjust**: Regularly monitor social media analytics to gain insights into the performance of your content and campaigns. Identify what is working well and what needs improvement. Use these insights to make data-driven decisions and adjust your strategy accordingly.

8. **Outsource or Delegate**: If you have the resources, consider outsourcing or delegating some social media tasks. Hiring a social media manager or working with a digital marketing agency can help alleviate the burden and ensure that social media activities are handled by experts.

9. **Stay Organized:** Maintain an organized system for storing and accessing your social media assets, such as images, videos, and graphics. Use content management tools or cloud storage

platforms to keep everything in one place and easily accessible when needed.

10. **Continuous Learning and Adaptation**: Stay up-to-date with the latest social media trends, algorithms, and best practices. Attend webinars, read industry blogs, and take courses to enhance your knowledge and skills. Social media is constantly evolving, so remaining adaptable and willing to learn is crucial for effective management.

By implementing these strategies, you can optimize your time and resources on social media, allowing you to achieve your goals efficiently and effectively. Remember, it's not about being present on every platform or constantly posting; it's about being strategic, engaging with your audience, and delivering valuable content that aligns with your objectives.

Staying Up-to-Date with the latest Social Media Trends and Features

In the ever-evolving landscape of social media, staying up-to-date with the latest trends and features is crucial to maintaining a competitive edge and maximizing your social media presence. By keeping abreast of the latest developments, you can leverage new opportunities, engage your audience effectively, and adapt your strategies accordingly. Here are some tips to help you stay up-to-date with the latest social media trends and features:

1. **Follow Industry Leaders and Influencers**: Identify key industry leaders, influencers, and experts in the field of social media marketing. Follow their blogs, social media accounts, and newsletters to receive insights, tips, and updates on emerging

trends. Their expertise and analysis can provide valuable guidance in navigating the ever-changing social media landscape.

2. **Join Social Media Communities and Groups**: Participate in social media communities and groups relevant to your industry or interests. Platforms like Facebook Groups and LinkedIn Groups offer opportunities to connect with like-minded professionals and enthusiasts. Engage in discussions, ask questions, and share knowledge to gain insights into the latest trends and features.

3. **Attend Webinars and Conferences**: Webinars and conferences focused on social media marketing are excellent resources for staying up-to-date. They often feature industry experts who provide in-depth analysis, case studies, and predictions about upcoming trends. Take advantage of these events to expand your knowledge, network with peers, and gain actionable insights.

4. **Subscribe to Newsletters and Publications**: Sign up for newsletters and publications that focus on social media marketing. These resources often deliver curated content, industry news, and updates directly to your inbox. Examples include Social Media Examiner, Social Media Today, and HubSpot's marketing newsletters. Regularly reading these publications will help you stay informed and inspired.

5. **Explore Official Social Media Blogs and Resources**: Social media platforms themselves are excellent sources of information. Subscribe to the official blogs and resources of platforms like Facebook, Instagram, Twitter, LinkedIn, and YouTube. These platforms often announce new features,

algorithm changes, and best practices directly, ensuring you're among the first to know.

6. **Engage in Continuous Learning**: Social media trends and features evolve rapidly, so it's crucial to adopt a mindset of continuous learning. Enroll in online courses, watch video tutorials, and read e-books focused on social media marketing. Platforms like LinkedIn Learning, Udemy, and Coursera offer a wide range of courses that can help you deepen your knowledge and skills.

7. **Experiment and Test New Features**: Social media platforms frequently introduce new features and tools to enhance user experiences. Stay curious and be willing to experiment with these features. Test how they can be incorporated into your social media strategy and assess their effectiveness. Be open to adapting your approach based on the results you observe.

8. **Monitor Competitors and Industry Benchmarks**: Keep an eye on your competitors' social media activities. Observe the strategies they employ, the content they share, and the features they utilize. Benchmark your performance against your competitors and industry leaders to identify areas for improvement and potential trends you may have overlooked.

9. **Engage with Your Audience**: Actively engage with your audience on social media platforms. Encourage them to share their feedback, preferences, and suggestions. Pay attention to their comments, questions, and concerns. Your audience can provide valuable insights into emerging trends and features they find appealing or expect from brands.

10. **Stay Tech-Savvy**: Social media platforms continually evolve their user interfaces and functionalities. Stay tech-savvy by familiarizing yourself with the latest platform updates, tools, and settings. Regularly explore the features available to you and experiment with different options to optimize your social media presence.

Implementing these strategies will make you can stay informed, adapt to changing trends, and leverage the latest features offered by social media platforms. Embrace a mindset of continuous learning, engage with industry experts, and be open to experimentation. Staying up-to-date will help you maintain a competitive advantage and ensure that your social media efforts remain relevant and effective.

Measuring and Analyzing your Social Media Performance

Measuring and analyzing your social media performance is crucial for understanding the effectiveness of your strategies, identifying areas for improvement, and making data-driven decisions. Let's explore some examples of metrics and analysis techniques that can help you assess and optimize your social media presence:

1. **Follower Growth**: Monitoring your follower growth provides insights into the appeal and reach of your social media profiles. For example, if you notice a significant increase in followers after implementing a specific content strategy, it indicates that your approach resonates with your target audience. On platforms like Instagram, you can track follower growth over time and analyze the impact of different campaigns or content themes.

2. Engagement Metrics: Engagements, such as likes, comments, shares, and retweets, demonstrate the level of interaction and interest in your content. Analyzing these metrics helps you understand what type of content captures your audience's attention. For instance, if you find that posts with video content receive higher engagement rates compared to text-based posts, you can prioritize video content in your future strategy.

3. Reach and Impressions: Reach and impressions provide insights into the visibility and exposure of your content. For example, on Facebook, you can track post reach to understand how many unique users saw your content. If you notice a decline in reach, it may indicate that algorithm changes or content adjustments are needed to regain visibility.

4. Referral Traffic and Conversions: Monitoring referral traffic from social media platforms to your website is crucial for assessing the impact of your social media efforts on driving website visitors. By using tools like Google Analytics, you can track the number of visitors, their behavior on your website, and conversions attributed to social media. For instance, you might find that Instagram drives a significant amount of traffic, but Twitter generates more conversions. This insight can help you allocate resources accordingly and optimize your conversion funnel.

5. Click-Through Rate (CTR): CTR measures the percentage of users who clicked on a link or call-to-action in your social media posts. It helps assess the effectiveness of your call-to-action and the relevance of your content. For instance, if you're promoting a blog post on Twitter and notice a low CTR, it may indicate the need to refine your messaging or make the link more prominent.

6. **Sentiment Analysis**: Analyzing the sentiment of comments and mentions can provide insights into how your audience perceives your brand or campaigns. Sentiment analysis tools can automatically categorize comments as positive, negative, or neutral. For example, if you launch a new product and notice a surge in positive sentiment, it indicates a successful product launch and positive reception.

7. **Competitor Analysis**: Benchmarking your performance against competitors helps you understand your position in the industry and identify areas for improvement. Analyze your competitors' follower growth, engagement rates, content themes, and campaigns. For instance, if a competitor consistently has higher engagement rates, you can study their content strategy and adapt it to fit your brand's voice and target audience.

8. **A/B Testing**: A/B testing involves creating multiple versions of a social media post or campaign and comparing their performance to determine the most effective approach. For example, you can test different visuals, headlines, or calls-to-action to see which variant generates higher engagement or click-through rates. A/B testing helps you make data-driven decisions by identifying the elements that resonate best with your audience.

9. **Audience Demographics**: Social media platforms provide insights into the demographic composition of your audience, such as age, gender, location, and interests. Analyzing this data helps you understand your target audience better and tailor your content to their preferences. For instance, if you discover that a significant portion of your audience consists of young

adults, you can create content that aligns with their interests and trends.

10. **Time and Day Analysis**: Analyzing the performance of your posts based on the time and day of publication can help optimize your content scheduling. By identifying the periods when your audience is most active and receptive, you can maximize the visibility and engagement of your posts. For example, if you find that your audience is more active on weekends, you can schedule important announcements or promotions during those times.

Remember, the choice of metrics and analysis techniques will depend on your specific goals and platforms. Regularly analyze your social media performance, iterate your strategies based on insights, and test new approaches to continually improve your social media presence.

Adapting your Strategy to Evolving Algorithms and Platform Changes

Social media platforms continuously update their algorithms and introduce changes that can significantly impact your organic reach, engagement, and overall performance. Adapting your strategy to these evolving algorithms and platform changes is crucial to maintaining a strong presence and maximizing your results. Here are some examples of how you can adapt your strategy:

1. **Understanding Algorithm Changes**: Stay informed about algorithm updates and changes announced by the social media platforms you use. For example, if Instagram announces a shift towards prioritizing Reels content, you can adapt your strategy

by incorporating more Reels into your content mix. By staying up to date, you can proactively adjust your tactics and leverage new features or formats that are favored by the algorithm.

2. **Diversifying Content Formats**: Experiment with different content formats to align with platform changes and user preferences. For instance, if a platform introduces a new feature like Stories or Live Video, incorporate these formats into your strategy to take advantage of their increased visibility and engagement potential. By diversifying your content, you can cater to different audience preferences and increase your chances of capturing attention in the evolving social media landscape.

3. **Prioritizing Meaningful Engagement**: Many platforms reward content that generates meaningful engagement. Instead of solely focusing on vanity metrics like likes or followers, emphasize generating thoughtful comments, shares, and discussions. For example, if Facebook's algorithm emphasizes "meaningful interactions," you can adapt your strategy by crafting posts that prompt users to share their opinions or ask open-ended questions to encourage conversations.

4. **Leveraging User-Generated Content (UGC):** User-generated content is highly valuable as it not only encourages engagement but also aligns with the authenticity and trustworthiness that platforms often prioritize. Encourage your audience to create and share content related to your brand or products. For instance, you can run contests or campaigns that encourage users to submit their own photos or videos showcasing how they use your products. UGC can help you maintain a consistent

flow of engaging content while leveraging the power of social proof.

5. Emphasizing Video Content: Video content continues to gain prominence across social media platforms. Platforms like Facebook, Instagram, and TikTok have introduced features that prioritize video content in users' feeds. Adapt your strategy by investing in video production and incorporating video content into your social media plan. For example, you can create tutorials, product demos, behind-the-scenes footage, or short-form entertaining videos to capture attention and boost engagement.

6. Exploring Influencer Partnerships: Influencers can have a significant impact on your social media performance, especially if they have a strong following and resonate with your target audience. Collaborating with influencers who align with your brand values can help you navigate algorithm changes and reach a wider audience. For instance, if a platform introduces features that boost content from verified or popular accounts, partnering with relevant influencers can increase your visibility and engagement.

7. Paid Advertising and Promoted Content: As organic reach becomes more challenging, consider incorporating paid advertising and promoted content into your strategy. Platforms offer various advertising options, such as Facebook Ads, Instagram Ads, Twitter Ads, and LinkedIn Ads. By allocating a portion of your budget to targeted advertising, you can amplify your reach, increase engagement, and achieve specific campaign objectives even amidst algorithm changes.

8. **Utilizing Analytics and Insights**: Regularly analyze the performance of your posts and campaigns using the analytics and insights provided by each platform. Look for patterns, trends, and correlations to understand what types of content or strategies are working best in the current algorithmic landscape. Adjust your content strategy based on these insights to optimize your performance. For example, if you find that video content consistently outperforms other formats, allocate more resources and effort towards video creation.

9. **Building a Strong Community:** Focus on building a loyal and engaged community around your brand. Platforms like Facebook and LinkedIn prioritize content from friends, family, and groups that users engage with frequently. By fostering a sense of community through active participation, responding to comments, and initiating discussions, you can increase the likelihood of your content being seen and engaged with by your community members.

10. **Staying Agile and Experimenting:** The social media landscape is ever-evolving, and what works today may not work tomorrow. Stay agile and be willing to experiment with new approaches, strategies, and content formats. Test different tactics, monitor the results, and iterate based on what resonates with your audience and performs well within the current algorithmic framework.

Adapting your strategy to evolving algorithms and platform changes requires a proactive and flexible approach. Stay informed, analyze data, experiment, and be willing to adjust your tactics to ensure your social media presence remains effective and aligned with the evolving dynamics of each platform.

Conclusion

Social media has revolutionized the way individuals and businesses connect, communicate, and engage with the world. It offers unparalleled opportunities for brand awareness, customer engagement, and business growth. By understanding the key strategies and insights discussed, you can harness the power of social media to its fullest potential.

First and foremost, measuring and analyzing your social media performance is essential. By tracking metrics such as follower growth, engagement rates, reach, and conversions, you gain valuable insights into what resonates with your audience and how to optimize your content strategy. Use this data to make informed decisions, refine your approach, and continuously improve your social media presence.

Adapting to evolving algorithms and platform changes is crucial for maintaining a strong presence. Stay informed about algorithm updates and changes, diversify your content formats, prioritize meaningful engagement, leverage user-generated content, and explore influencer partnerships. Embracing video content, utilizing paid advertising, and building a strong community are also effective strategies to navigate algorithmic shifts and maximize your reach and impact.

Furthermore, analytics and insights are your allies. Regularly analyze your performance, identify trends, and use data-driven insights to guide your decision-making. Experiment, stay agile, and be willing to adapt your tactics to align with the ever-changing social media landscape.

In conclusion, embracing the power of social media requires an active and strategic approach. By applying the knowledge gained from measuring and analyzing your performance, adapting to algorithmic changes, leveraging diverse content formats, and utilizing analytics, you can unlock the full potential of social media for your personal brand or business. Embrace the opportunities it offers, experiment with new strategies, and engage with your audience authentically. Take action today and harness the immense power of social media to propel your success in the digital age.

ABOUT THE AUTHOR

Kay Julius is a seasoned expert in the realm of social media, with a passion for helping individuals and businesses harness the power of digital platforms to achieve extraordinary results. With an extensive background in social media management and marketing, Kay has accumulated a wealth of knowledge and hands-on experience in building large and engaged followings across various social media platforms.

Having successfully built and managed social media pages with followers numbering in the millions, Kay has demonstrated an exceptional understanding of what it takes to cultivate a thriving online community. From starting from scratch and growing followers organically to implementing strategic tactics for accelerated growth, Kay has mastered the art of capturing attention, fostering engagement, and creating meaningful connections in the digital landscape.

Kay has collaborated with numerous brands and individuals, ranging from startups to established organizations, helping them establish a powerful presence on social media. By applying a unique blend of creativity, strategic thinking, and data-driven insights, Kay has consistently delivered outstanding results, propelling brands and individuals to new levels of visibility, influence, and success.

Beyond the realm of social media management, Kay is a dedicated educator and mentor. Recognizing the transformative impact of social media, Kay has made it a mission to share knowledge and empower others to navigate the ever-evolving digital landscape. Through workshops, speaking engagements, and online resources, Kay has inspired countless individuals to seize the opportunities presented by social media and unleash their full potential.

With a deep understanding of the nuances and intricacies of various social media platforms, Kay is at the forefront of industry trends and best practices. From Facebook to Instagram, Twitter to YouTube, Kay possesses a comprehensive understanding of each platform's unique features and optimization strategies.

As an author, Kay brings together his wealth of experience, insights, and practical guidance in this book on social media following. This comprehensive guide is a testament to Kay's dedication to helping others navigate the complex world of social media and unlock the immense benefits it offers.